A Lion's Hunt

A Lion's Hunt

HEARTBREAK DOESN'T
BREAK YOUR HEART.
IT BREAKS YOUR GUT.

Roberto Sanchez Jr.

Charleston, SC
www.PalmettoPublishing.com

A Lion's Hunt
Copyright © 2023 by Roberto Sanchez Jr.

All rights reserved

No portion of this book may be reproduced, stored in a retrieval system, or transmitted in any form by any means—electronic, mechanical, photocopy, recording, or other—except for brief quotations in printed reviews, without prior permission of the author.

Paperback ISBN: 979-8-8229-1136-9
eBook ISBN: 979-8-8229-1137-6

Table of Contents

Introduction vii
Chapter 1   The Real Truth about Why Opposites Attract 1
Chapter 2   What It Truly Means to Beg Someone 5
Chapter 3   Adding Value after a Breakup Will Only Increase
            Your Frequency 7
Chapter 4   Your Daily Rituals Determine the Result of Your
            New Relationship 10
Chapter 5   True Love Is a Routine 12
Chapter 6   Gen Z Makes Our Job Easy 14
Chapter 7   The Honeymoon Phase Never Dies 18
Chapter 8   Subconsciously Your Present Competes with
            Your Past 21
Chapter 9   The Score Is Even Now 25
Chapter 10 Comforting Their Behavior 27
Chapter 11 Why Closure between Two People Is Important
            after a Breakup 29
Chapter 12 Why Your Ex Keeps Coming Back 32
Chapter 13 When You Prioritize Your Insecurities 34
Chapter 14 Tolerance Is One Thing, but Tolerance and
            Self-Respect Are Another 36
About the Author 38

Introduction

As I grew up, I was always told that a lion is a great example of authority and respect because he is the king of the jungle and has massive sheer power. I always wanted to represent that statue. I loved the idea that every single animal respects and fears him. His roar says it all. I understood then and there why every animal fears him. The more I saw videos of a lion hunting his prey or defeating his enemies, the more I understood why he is the king of the jungle.

One day I saw this particular video of the lion battling his archenemy—the hyena. I could not believe my eyes from what I just saw. Humanlike behavior. I could relate to that behavior so much. But how can this be? He's an animal, and I'm a human. I don't hunt for my food; I purchase it. Even if I would, I would eat it because I hunted and worked for it. Those were my younger beliefs and thoughts. But little did I know that because of my old mindset, I wasn't the king of my jungle. What the lion did was hunt down the matriarch of the hyenas and tore it apart in front of its clan. When he was done with her, he simply walked away, even though he was hungry. Like I said, my old belief system would have eaten my meal that I had hunted for or worked for. But the lion's mentality does not work that way. The lion every now and then has to show everyone around him why he is the king of the jungle, not to survive but to prove all those that doubt him and his power.

Overall, the lion loves the hunt. He enjoys the process. He loves the hunt more than the destination, while we humans love to get to the destination before we enjoy the process of getting there. So? A lion's hunt is what these chapters indicate for you to apply in your relationships. For you to enjoy and understand the process of your very own relationship. For you to not say, "Until we get married, that's when our relationship will get better." Don't, because your relationship will not get better until you enjoy and endure the hardships with your significant other. During the tribulations/chaos, you have to show your loved one why you chose them and give them that constant reminder. It's not about making it; it's about maintaining your successful relationship. How do you do that? You take these chapters with the thought, That's a good way of looking at it, and those are great perspectives, and if my relationship is on the rocks, then I need to apply *A Lion's Hunt* mentality to my love life.

CHAPTER 1

The Real Truth about Why Opposites Attract

"Date someone that is the opposite of you. Because if you date someone who's exactly like you, then you will be finding yourself in an argument every single time." When I heard this, I took it very seriously, and my perspective of it was that if I found a girl who was the complete opposite of me, then that meant there was a future there and a promising one. That the relationship would last till the end of our days. Because of that belief, whenever I found myself going on dates with girls and started seeing similarities between us, I would start to see red flags all over. So I went ahead with that perspective. In high school all the girls around me were all very alike to me. So I couldn't see them as my lovers. Subconsciously, my mind attracted a girl from a different high school and with different thoughts and beliefs. There she was, the perfect and ideal girl because she was the opposite of me. She went to a different high school, she dressed differently, and she carried herself differently from the ones in my high school. So I went for it. Subconsciously, my mind went for it.

We dated, and sure enough our worlds were very different. I showed her a world full of partying, and she showed me a world full of adventure and culture. But as our relationship went on, we seemed to have very similar personalities. Next thing we knew, arguments arose, and we both acted on pride and didn't talk for weeks. Eventually, the storm came to its end. Our lives came back to its normal state of well-being. But no relationship is perfect, and again, the clouds caved in on us. Pride was the winner. I started to realize that inwardly we were very alike and that our outside worlds were very opposite. So that was the answer to all my doubts and confusion—that you can both have opposite worlds and benefit from it, showing each other different worlds and causing excitement and new horizons. It makes it exciting and fun. That's why you always see the bad boy in high school end up with the sweet, innocent girl. But that doesn't mean that it will work out to the end of their days and flourish because again, they are opposites outwardly and the exact same inwardly. Now if their outside worlds are completely different or as in it the same and have opposite personalities, then it will most certainly work out.

As I went through my breakup with my high school sweetheart Diana, I stumbled into a girl who was forever going to change my life around but more than anything explain to me why we would work out until our end of days. And so there she was, your beautiful blond Latina who would demand attention from all who would cross her path because of her insanely good looks. I remember how enjoyable it was to stare at her. Opposite worlds for sure. She lived in Ann Arbor, a rich city in Michigan, and graduated from Michigan State University. She came from a loving home, while I lived in a dirt-poor city, was a college dropout, and came from a broken home. Very different worlds for sure. She became my girlfriend eventually after we showed each other our opposite worlds.

As our relationship went on, we had our problems and many breakups, but this time it was different. When we would fight, I would hold my pride up so high, but she wouldn't. To my surprise the problem was resolved in a matter of hours. It didn't take weeks or months. It was so amazing to see this but so confusing because of what I was used to with my ex-girlfriend Diana. But why? Because Pamela didn't carry pride or prioritize it. Yet she prioritized resentment when I would fall short with her, and I did not. I could not resent someone for long, especially the love of my life. Yet she could. But that was OK because that was where I came in and balanced out our love life. So inwardly we were opposites in that area, but we managed to keep our relationship strong and healthy. I was a dreamer, while she was a logical person. I was at the gym for hours, while she was back home picking out an outfit for our date night. She was all about maintaining her credit score high and clean, while I was saying, "Cash is king." I was a risk-taker, while she played it safe. We were the yin and yang. It all made sense to me. Pamela and I were opposites inwardly as well as outwardly. Diana and I were opposites outwardly but so similar inwardly.

All in all, what it comes down to is this: Outwardly you both can live in completely different worlds. But inwardly if you both have differences with your beliefs and same persona, then you both will outweigh each other, and one disagreement will give and make the relationship blossom. Now outwardly you can have the exact same outside world as them, but if you both have the same exact similarities in beliefs and personalities, then those beliefs and personalities will not outweigh each other for you both to move forward. That's the one thing that will set your romantic relationship up for failure. Pamela didn't carry pride the way I did, so it benefited the relationship to move forward. Diana carried pride the same exact way I did, so it hindered the relationship. Pamela wanted to be the alpha in our relationship because of a trend. Yet I am an alpha and naturally wanted to lead our relationship and did. Diana was a spiritual woman, and so was I, whereas Pamela was not. But that was where I came into the picture and carried the team. But if Diana was a spiritual woman and so was I, then there was only one room for an alpha to lead that role. That's where conflicts would arise. Yet if Pamela wanted guidance and desired a spiritual life, then I could give that to her and, most importantly, lead.

That's where we both would be opposite. So it balanced itself out and made the relationship move forward.

To be opposites both outwardly and inwardly is one great thing and will set a relationship to blossom, but to be opposites outwardly and similar inwardly is where the confusion lies. That is where the chaos resides.

CHAPTER 2

What It Truly Means to Beg Someone

To beg someone for their love and know your worth at the same time is like winning the lottery. The majority of people perceive begging as a bad thing—almost like degrading yourself. The reality is it's not. In a different world of perception, it is showing her affection and love. It's not degrading yourself, and it isn't not knowing your value. Begging someone but knowing your worth is an act of bravery and conviction. Because when she rejects you, that can't hurt you. It's like your shield. Because what protects you is your sense of worth. So every time she rejects you, it has to go through your sense of worth first. That will be the knowledge that will be taking all these hits—not your emotions. So the people who do not know their worth don't have that shield. Therefore, rejections attack their emotions directly without any protection. Knowing your worth equals confidence, standing your ground.

The same thing applies when you pick her up from her parents' house when you first start dating. Are you that type who gets out of the car to meet the parents and ask permission for their daughter to go out? Or are you the type who gets there and texts her the classic "Here"?—meaning you don't have that confidence to go up to that door because you're scared of rejection? And most of all, you don't have that shield to protect your emotions. So because you act on the emotion of fear and not on the knowledge of knowing your worth, you lose. Fear is not real; danger is very real.

All in all if you harness this mentality, you will prove to yourself and others why you are a millennial, why millennials are mentally stronger than Gen Z, why we tolerate and endure more hurt and rejection. It's because we were raised with a hard hand. We were raised with discipline. The majority of our lifetime as kids was never given instant gratification compared with Gen Z today, which has made them weaker in the area of love and courage. The fact that they are doing less and less actions to show love to the person they want to date, the more that I stay true to how valuable my actions are in showing a woman love (begging her) and to date her. This is why Gen Zers make my job easy. I stand out now more than ever, which is a great thing for us millennials because when we were kids, we knew that we needed to use the training wheels on our bikes first before we could ride them without falling. We were willing to fail first without even knowing it. Gen Zers don't have this mentality. They want instant success, but success takes time.

This is one of the many secrets to getting a high-maintenance girl. This is why Gen Zers make my job easy.

CHAPTER 3

Adding Value after a Breakup Will Only Increase Your Frequency

There have always been two choices you are left with after you are faced with a breakup: either you get up or stay there to suffer. The moment you make the decision to increase your frequency instead of letting it be stagnant, you are creating new opportunities with other frequencies that are in that same state of frequency. The higher you go, the more new horizons you will discover. But if you don't, then you will just keep attracting what you already know, which is the same frequency as your ex. Adding value to yourself after a breakup is a powerful tool. More than anything, it is the escape from your continuous suffering after she has left and moved on.

The reality is that in this world, we have been domesticated to suffer. Majority of the people after a breakup, instead of bettering themselves in areas they need to grow in or get better in, they do the opposite. They run to pleasure to end the pain. When you were never taught that you're human and you're allowed to feel, in order to become stronger, you have to feel the pain for you to grow and know what that's like. Once you have been in pain, if you go through that pain again, it won't hurt as much as it did the first time. Why? Because your emotions have been there before.

That's the beauty of life and being a human being. Like the saying "What doesn't kill you makes you stronger," so more than anything we as humans are addicted to suffering because that's the easy route out. We as humans and our brains have been wired to avoid pain and obstacles when in reality we should welcome pain. That is the very thing that's going to elevate us to the best version of ourselves.

Anyone can take my advice with the ladies. For example, when I say you have to know when to walk away, some of you can take this advice and apply it to yourself. But if you have no value, it does not work. It's useless.

Now the question here is, "But why does it not work? If you succeeded with it, why can't I? It's the same formula." Yes, it is the same formula, but are you willing to sacrifice what I was when I was in the process—in the way of being aware of your worth? Most importantly you have to know how powerful and how fulfilling investing in yourself can be.

So here it is. When someone is seeking help in this journey, it's important to know that it's a process to get where you want to be. That being said, there's no shortcut to this, no magic button. What lies in between you and that girl you desperately want is creating value in yourself. For example, it may be gaining muscle, gaining knowledge, learning time management, learning new hobbies, learning a good sense of humor, or learning self-discipline. All these will create the act of self-love. These improvements will bring joy, peace, and love into your life. Once you have that, you will attract that girl. This is the insight and advice for it to work. It will only work for you if you create that high value in yourself.

Now the insight into why this works is because when you say, "Enough is enough," when they have treated you in such a way that they want to, then you walk away. For some time they will not miss you because the reality is your frequency was very low at that time. But now that you walked away and did your homework and you started to add frequency to your higher self, what happens? They start to feel your absence. They truly do.

People will mention your name and start to talk about how much you have changed after the breakup. It will become a word-of-mouth thing. She will start to realize what she is losing, as opposed to someone who did not add value to themselves after the breakup. With that type of person, she's not losing much except their company. She won't feel that because she has felt that frequency when they were in the relationship already. What is there to miss? What's new? Nothing. But if you add value in yourself, then, my friend, there will be something to miss—something they have not felt or seen in you.

CHAPTER 4

Your Daily Rituals Determine the Result of Your New Relationship

I remember having a mentee while I was in my process. His name was Paco. He admired me so much. So one day I made the choice to take him under my wing and guide him because I couldn't stand to see him suffering. He was desperate for answers in his personal love life. It's more accurate to say his love life sucked. He was going out there on dates but always ended up with no results. What could he possibly be doing wrong? He was a good-looking guy. He had a lot going for him. Well, at least I assumed that. As I entered his world and got more insights into his lifestyle, I realized that his rituals were dull and boring. He had no hobbies that would entertain someone else who entered his world and lifestyle. He did not have rituals of self-discipline that lead to self-love, rituals that garner people's praise and admiration.

There's this quote that states, "If you are not changing someone else's life, you are wasting your time." People will be attracted to you for many reasons. When someone is attracted to you for one of your discipline rituals, that's it—game over. Why? Because that ritual is part of you, and discipline is an act of self-love. Discipline is something you cannot ever pretend to be because discipline takes effort. They will see that that's part of your lifestyle, and it will be contagious to them. Before you know it, they have entered a new world of self-love. Subconsciously, they become more like you, and subconsciously, they come to an agreement to adopt these self-improvement rituals and hobbies because unconsciously they are in a better place, meaning they feel it more than they are aware of it. So they feel that they are in a much better place than when they were without you. You have officially invited them into your world.

Now the question remains: Is your world self-improving, captivating, promising, and fun? Or is it boring with no self-growth? When the person sees no future there, they leave. Then you go about your life and go on to the next person with the same rituals, and you are left wondering why you keep getting left on *Read* in your personal messages. If you continue on with the same rituals, then you will end up with the same result. But if you adopt new and exciting rituals, then the person who steps into your life will hang around longer and make it a permanent stay.

CHAPTER 5

True Love Is a Routine

Routine is everything, if you think about it, when it comes to a breakup. You've invested quite some time in this person you call your love. Am I wrong? Your Saturday nights were dedicated to that significant other—maybe even the whole weekend. You have walked into their lives and, most of all, their world.

So this is what leads me to what my whole point here is: to be stubborn and loyal to your routine even when you step into your significant other's routine is what will make all the difference after they have left you heartbroken. Say you were in a serious relationship, and one day that person decides to walk out of your life—tells you it's not you, it's them, so don't take anything personally. That person is absent now, aren't they? The days that you would go over for a game night at their parents' house will no longer be. The sweet sixteen party you would go to every Friday because that person had such a big family—those are over too. The love of the routine is what kept the relationship as strong as could be. So now you're left without a routine. You have lived in their routine for so long that you have forgotten yours before that person walked into your life. It's been so long that you can't even remember it because you no longer were in love with your routine but theirs. Think about it. Before you met that person, you had your very own that you loved and adored. At that moment no one could take it from you but you, which was not going to happen because that routine is yours until you decide something different. Then you understand in order to move on, you need to recreate a routine that you will eventually fall in love with again. To understand this when this is happening, then you will be at peace and have a sense of direction. And so they say when you know what you want, that's everything.

See, where we fail is when we don't keep our very own routine even when another one steps into ours. It's crucial to keep your routine because people change and will take back their routine whenever they desire it. They won't take it back physically but mentally and most of all by being absent in your life the moment you break up. This is the key when you go at it alone again. Because the reality is you came into this world alone, and you will leave this world alone. In life there are always those two words: better or worse, meaning that when two individuals get together, they become as one whole. All your routines and beliefs will come together. But there is so much room for everything. Eventually, things have to give.

Subconsciously, we lean most on the best and more convenient habits because we all want the best for ourselves. This is true. So if you know that routine makes you the best version of yourself, then you will harness it for yourself and the relationship. You agree to this without even knowing it. It is said you don't really know when you fall in love with someone. But the reality is if you know this, then you will realize why you have fallen in love with that person. All in all you really fall in love with them because their routine in life has benefited you and made you a better version of yourself. You have fallen for that person's routine because now it's yours. Now that person is part of you. That person has taken you out of your misery—if that's what your routine felt like. That's why they say someone walks into your life to show you why it didn't work out with your past. And those reasons are because your present routine defeats the old one; you have witnessed both routines, and only you know which one is more convenient to you and to your well-being.

CHAPTER 6

Gen Z Makes Our Job Easy

In my journey of chasing a high-caliber girl, I realized a lot. To my surprise I discovered a great insight in love that could change the game for the old school. I always set myself apart from the rest, so I knew I was different. Something in me would always cry out to rebel if I ever decided to act like the rest—so I never did. And for those of you who don't get this feeling, then it's as simple as believing it, then you can at least start to see it. This is important because for what I am about to share, it's essential that you feel this way so you can act on it. Even for those who aren't old school, you can be that or be as close as possible to that. So you could obtain the result of this avatar.

As I chased her, I took the actions that at the moment I thought were the best. These actions came out of confidence. They never stemmed from fear or insecurities. That was what made all the difference. So as I went on in my journey, every Friday I gave her roses, gifts, and letters. I wanted her to know that she was worthy of love, that everything that I was doing was what she deserved—I believe that and more, really.

So my final gift to her was to keep my promise, which at the time was for me to go to Mexico and show up at her doorsteps of her little town, to prove to her what I was capable of. I think at that point it wasn't even about getting her to date me again. Really, at that point all I wanted was to make my vision and promise a reality. I wanted to prove to myself that if it was meant to be, it was up to me. Of course, in the back of my head, my expectation was for her to fall head over heels for me when she saw that I had made it. But to all our surprise, it didn't happen that way.

I came, I saw, I conquered. Before I knew it, my vision and promise had come to reality. I think it was a turning point in my life. My faith and belief that you could have whatever you want had grown so immensely! It changed my life forever.

After my arrival to her little town in Mexico, she welcomed me to stay and enjoy New Year's with her and her family. At that point you would think I would be bitter and have resentment. Because if I came all the way from Detroit, Michigan, to a little town close to Mexico City in a car, then she must have said yes to me and said, "I am all yours." But the reality was that wasn't the result. Before I made this choice, I told myself that my expectations were not to get her to date me once more. My intention was more focused on proving myself and showing myself what I was capable of doing. That was what made all the difference.

I can admit that rejection sucks. When it all comes down to it, I am a human just like you. I was left heartbroken after New Year's of 2019. But after all of this, I still wished her the best and left on a good note. I didn't leave on bad terms because I'm smart enough to know that all that causes resentment and bad energy. Yet I found myself with a broken heart back home. Weeks passed by after my journey. And then she texted me, saying the unthinkable: that she was wrong this whole time. That she wanted a second shot at love again—but this time with me. My mind was distraught. I couldn't help but feel so much love and joy inside me. But I won't lie—I did hesitate when I got the text. But because I knew that if I acted on resentment or getting back at her, these behaviors would lead to bad frequencies, which I had committed to never act on—to kill them with kindness. And so I did. I killed her with kindness. And the rest is history.

So why does Gen Z make our job easy in making a ten fall in love with us? The job to date a high-maintenance girl. The simple fact that Gen Z does not take rejection well, and more than anything, they give conditional love. They don't know what unconditional love is. To my awareness she told me everything that happened after I left and during my absence. Guys were trying to get with her left and right. I couldn't blame them. She's a ten, for crying out loud. I always told her a girl like her won't go unnoticed for long. I was right. But it never led to anything else. And lastly, she had met up with her ex-boyfriend. She had told herself, "Well, if all guys are the same, then I might as well go back to what I know." Plus, she already had so much invested in her past relationship with her ex-boyfriend. So it was OK for her.

Yet my actions of being old school said different. The force of the power of love that I had because I was old school and I loved in the old-school way had made all the difference—because I was willing to do what they weren't willing to do for her. My actions and my behavior toward love spoke louder than words! For me it was natural because I loved doing this. I found excitement in every act of love that I did for her. So this is the secret:harness the avatar of being old school. When I speak of being old school, what I mean is giving love to the person you are trying to date but giving it unconditionally, not conditionally. Unconditional love is giving your love without any conditions. Love that is pure and sincere. That is why conditional love is very toxic. That's what separates conditional love from unconditional love—unconditional love is natural when conditional love is forced and with terms in it.

Nowadays, in this new generation, it seems no one wants to get hurt. So that's why they act on conditional love, because they want the love guaranteed. But little do Gen Z know that love is not meant to be forced but meant to come naturally and purely without any conditions. If it doesn't come naturally to you in giving unconditional love, I want you to know that it's possible because I did it. That way you will set yourself apart from the rest and obtain that girl you always dreamed of.

CHAPTER 7

The Honeymoon Phase Never Dies

Love is so important to us. I think at the end of the day, everything that we do is for love, really. Think about it. Whatever short-term goal or long-term goal you're chasing, what's the result of it? When I was chasing my fiance and she wanted nothing to do with me, I literally dropped everything for her. I really did. I took a whole month off work. I had money saved up, ready for whatever could happen. I neglected everyone in my life at that moment. I bought a car, cashed out on it, and drove from Michigan all the way to southern Mexico alone because I was on a mission. Well, more to say I was in *A Lion's Hunt*. The terminology of *A Lion's Hunt* derives from the lion himself and what he represents. It was what led me to the title of my very own book—*A Lion's Hunt*.

The journey that I explain in this book is what started it all for me and more than anything made me realize that if you adopt this mentality, nothing can hurt you, not even rejection from the girl you are pursuing. I remember that journey so well. I felt invincible and with so much joy. I was the happiest person alive. I felt that. I could honestly say I was the richest man alive because I had a dream: to arrive at a destination I had no address for, to know that I had to figure it out myself, and most of all to put all my energy on faith and God himself. I had to rely on him to give me a sense of direction—which he did.

A year has passed since that event. It's been a good year and hell of a ride. I must say I'm definitely in a different place now. It feels different. I have my fiancée next to me. But things don't feel like they once did a year ago. When I was in *A Lion's Hunt*, I could state that a year ago I was in my honeymoon phase with her—the phrase all the love experts say occurs in the beginning of every relationship. I always wondered if this theory was true.

I have to admit these past months with her have been hell—very stressful. But why? Has she stopped growing? The biggest question of all was, was the honeymoon phase over? Then I started to self-reflect just yesterday. I realized this was all a lie—to my demise! The honeymoon phase is real! But when disrespect starts to happen in your relationship, that is the key word here that destroys and hinders the honeymoon phase.

The honeymoon phase is very much alive—until that person begins to lose respect for you. When speaking of respect, it comes in so many ways. The two major ones are verbally and physically. They are considered abuse. But because there is someone else involved, they are first and foremost disrespectful—disrespect to degrade you and make you feel less, disrespect to put their hands on you when they can't control their own anger and emotions. It's like having a ticking time bomb. It will destroy whatever it's close to.

I started to notice these past few days I had no urgency to get up from bed and surprise her anymore—or even randomly show up at her door with some roses. Because that's what the honeymoon phase does to you—it makes you do these things. Yet I wasn't there anymore. Now the question is, can it come back? Can we be at that place we once were?

This question applies to two types of couples. The first is soulmates. It never really dies for them. It's just hindered by disrespect. But the moment you apply respect back to that romantic relationship, then it repairs itself on its own. The second is the ones who aren't soulmates—the couples. The answer is distance. You need to get away from each other—with respect, of course—for you both to appreciate and miss each other. Most of all it's important for you to find it in yourself to forgive and be grateful that you both have another opportunity to reclaim your honeymoon phase.

CHAPTER 8

Subconsciously Your Present Competes with Your Past

Whenever we get ourselves in a new relationship, we are unconsciously making an agreement with the other person. That agreement states why they are better than your past or why they won't cut it. Until they prove to you why they are better, that's when you're unconsciously falling more and more in love with them. They have a scorecard just as you do. You just don't know it.

So without us knowing, we are constantly comparing the new relationship with the old one because that's the only one we have known for quite some time now. I remember a couple of months back in my relationship with my fiance—this was when we were dating—she always hinted at me about her car issues. So in my head I knew what she was hinting at. I just always found myself procrastinating about it. I think it was much easier to do that because it wasn't mine. That never meant that I didn't love her. But my actions said different things—until we got into a big argument, and she let out all the feelings she was suppressing. She found herself speaking about how I never changed her car oil or checked it and that she was so used to her past man doing that for her. So right then and there, I knew I was losing because I wasn't beating him at his game. I wasn't living up to that expectation of what she was used to.

If I had caught this, it was my duty to do that but better. I had to keep scoring points in her love language. So I took it upon myself to improve that. I knew if I did that little thing, I would score in her love language. Competition isn't an easy thing to execute. It has to become a habit of yours you keep plucking away at until you get it just right. So yet again I found myself catching these scorecards playing out. I saw it before my own eyes again.

But this time it was different. This time it was my birthday. When it comes to my birthday, I don't ask for much, really, especially with gifts. I would rather my significant other not buy me anything. I'd rather have an awesome home-cooked meal, really. So I woke up like usual—always the first one out of bed. (I consider myself an early bird.) So I went about my rituals and got my coffee so I could start writing. Yet I heard nothing in the kitchen, no sound of someone getting out of the bed. I got no hug or great gesture. Nothing. In some weird way, I felt alone. It's so hard to admit this. But it felt this way. So I got up and left to go run some errands. When I left, it was hitting the afternoon. Yet I got back home, and there was no one—no food or surprise. I went and opened the closed doors in all the rooms, just maybe hoping she would be there with balloons and waiting for me to open that door so she could surprise me. At least that was my expectation. Yet nothing. I had one last hope. That was the kitchen. Maybe there would lie my high expectation and surprise I'd been dying for. Again, nothing.

I couldn't take it or believe it. I started to get anxiety and took it upon myself to leave so maybe I could find that relief I was so dying for. So I packed my stuff and left and hopped on the freeway back to Detroit.

I started to get calls from her, so I pulled over. Yet I couldn't reply. I was too hurt, really. To my surprise she kept insisting, but this time she sent me pictures of what she had bought to celebrate my birthday. She had my gift ready. She had picked up my cake and bought everything she needed to make my favorite breakfast. I guess by that time it was too late. The damage had been done already.

So was that it? Was it that I didn't have the patience to wait around to see what would happen? To my awareness it wasn't that. The reality was that in my past birthdays with my past partner, she had been very dedicated and loving when it came to my birthday. She would be up before me. She would have asked for the day off from work if she had to because she knew it was my day. She knew it was my special day. It wasn't about the gifts for me. It was about the intention and nurture she gave when my special day came around. So then and there, I realized that unconsciously Pam (my Fiance) was competing with Diana (my ex-girlfriend). But Pam lost in my scorecard because Diana had done it just right—with so much care. Yet Pam did it when it was convenient for her—unfortunately. This didn't mean she didn't love me because I know she does. It's just that we don't know of this insight—how it works and what to do when this arises. I have come to a realization of this because I went through it, not because someone gave me this advice. I lived it—in person and on my birthday.

But a question remained lingering in the back of my mind—till this day, really. Why was it that I couldn't reach my dream physique with my high school sweetheart? But yet when we left each other's side, I was a force to be reckoned with. Nothing could stop me but the force of love. I didn't understand that until my new relationship walked in through those doors and had taught me why. Not that they literally tell me why. I had to go through it to understand why.

As I went on with my new relationship, every behavior she did to me or said to me was competing with my past behavior and language. In a big, great way, my past had created these standards for me because she had left so many imprints within my body but most of all within my mind. Automatically, this was wired to happen no matter what. The person didn't matter or who they were, but their actions and words did. If my present decided to disrespect me or get out of line, guess what. My past was there to tell me "Remember what I would do? I would have never done that because I wouldn't forgive myself and make you feel that way. See? This is how I would have done it. Do you remember, Roberto? Whenever I would do anything for you, it was out of respect but most of all because it made you happy. So I kept it that way, Roberto. I kept it that way because I love you. And that is what love is."

So there it was, her voice lingering in my head every time my present would do the opposite. It had become a warfare in my mind that would hinder me and my present relationship. Well, if you looked at it the victim way. But if you would look at it the opposite way, then there was something valuable to be learned about this event in my life. So I did just that every time. But as I did that every time, there was always friction in my mind. It came to a point where I didn't want it anymore. It was so exhausting and wearing down my present and me. Unfortunately, when you step into this awareness of it more to say your conscious mind knows about this and then stores it in your subconscious mind, it's an imprint forever.

CHAPTER 9

The Score Is Even Now

I remember this day so vividly and clearly—almost as if I looked down at my body and stared at my tattoos. I believe that when you remember something so clearly, it's because you're very passionate about it or it's something at that moment that is very important to you. To me it was really analyzing what went wrong and connecting the dots. Because that's what I love to do—connect dots and end up with a solution to help the rest and have answers for myself and my own well-being.

So that day was a good old day: I got home from work and, well, came home to my fiance. Well, at the time she was my girlfriend. But we got in an argument—a pretty deep one! And I was pretty upset about this whole situation, enough that I raised my voice at her. Well, I yelled at her. She cried—quite a lot! It was almost as if no one had ever made her cry before. But in her eyes it was basically that. So she cried to me that not even her parents or her ex-boyfriend would ever raise their voice at her.

I laughed. I didn't laugh like the usual laugh I put out into the world—that laugh that is so obnoxious. But it was the type of laugh that is subtle and carries a facial expression in it. That was because to me it was too clear. I understood everything. I understood why she saw it that way and why I saw it a very different way. I responded and told her that I knew why. That I knew why her ex-boyfriend never raised his voice at her.

There are many reasons a person in a relationship will not yell at you or try to get even with you after you have disrespected them or behaved in a disrespectful manner. The ones that I experienced are the following. The first is guilt because they have done something worse or have done something in the past that makes them feel conscious and guilty inside. By this I mean they have acted on a bad habit that would jeopardize the relationship. Because they know if the partner finds out, it's the end of that relationship. So to them if they keep quiet and tolerate their behavior, then the score is even. "I did something bad, so they just did me bad, but it's OK because I did something bad too." It's their guilty conscience that tells them not to panic because they have done the same or worse.

The second one is not knowing your self-worth—to have fear that if you fight for what you believe, then that person will leave you because they don't agree with it. But because you don't know your self-worth, you choose to silence your thoughts and beliefs. Because you fear the breakup. You fear that you will never do better. You fear rejection and being alone for the rest of your life. But if you truly knew the truth that once you tap into your conscious mind and discover your self-worth, then you would know that you could have whatever it is you want in this world. That is because we are made up of energy. If you work on yourself, then your energy will go up and skyrocket. That eventually you will resonate another energy at that level. And if you both make an agreement, then both of your energy frequencies will collide and unite as a whole. That, my friend, is what we call love or a new relationship. That's when we begin to say to others, "Oh, we broke up. But I have found someone new."

CHAPTER 10

Comforting Their Behavior

Comforting someone's behavior derives from what we don't do after someone has done us wrong. It's very different behavior than what we are used to doing after someone does us wrong—almost like when a child keeps stealing from a grocery store, and we reward them for it. When comforting their behavior comes into play, it is when you show them compassion and empathy. This would mean not acting negatively once the child has stolen but lecturing them about why it's wrong with a positive attitude. So that's what is comforting that behavior.

Now in the love language, it's like this. When we're with our significant other, we at times have the tendency to want to check their phones or social media, perhaps because of their behavior as of late. This happened to me once. My significant other judged me for going through her phone. But why? Why did she make me feel bad about it? Was it the fact that she was judging me for my behavior? Or could she have been so caught up with being right instead of comforting me and being understanding? Because I know I have done that with her when she has done that to me. When it came to me, I just laughed and did not resist it. But when it came to her phone, she had a cow.

I truly believe one thing that I have captured here is that when someone makes a mistake or is in the wrong, it's very important for the significant other to reassure them it's OK and to prove to them that what they are thinking is all a misunderstanding, and overall, they understand why and have empathy for them. It's almost like when you grieve—you have to be allowed to do that for you to be at peace. If you suppress your feelings, then you're only hurting yourself. The same thing goes with ranting—you're not looking for an answer but a shoulder to cry on. That's it. That you understand why they behaved in such a way—that they had all the right to behave the way they did. Because initially our behavior caused that to happen. Our past made an imprint on them that led them to behave that way they did with our phone. If I behaved in a very anxious and angry way with them after they started to go through my phone, then it was for a reason. Because if I had nothing to hide, I would be at peace with it and OK with it. But the opposite is also true: if I were hiding something in my phone, then I wouldn't want my significant other to find out because I know it would damage our relationship. So as a defense mechanism, I make them feel guilty for what they are doing.

CHAPTER 11

Why Closure between Two People Is Important after a Breakup

I had dated my ex for eight years of my life until everything came spiraling down. By that I mean the end of our relationship. This was not your normal type of breakup. It wasn't a toxic one—I didn't cheat or physically abuse her. And the same goes for her. I think what this breakup meant to me was temporary, but most of all it was a challenge—a challenge to see what I was capable of doing on my own without her. I have always been a person who wanted to be the best version of myself as far back as I can remember.

So I moved on into this world of the unknown. I had decided to become uncomfortable. They say, "Get comfortable with the uncomfortable." I didn't understand that back then. But the moment I captured this insight and the secret of life, I understood it so well. It's the law of life.

I ended our relationship through a text. Some can say that wasn't too smart. Yes, but the opposite is also true. At that moment of my life, I did not know what I was getting myself into, really.

The two things that kept me pushing forward with this decision were faith and love—the love for myself, which also falls in the category of confidence, because self-discipline is an act of self-love.

After that we never talked. Eight months passed. Christmas came around. Gosh, it was a lonely one. New Year's came around. Gosh, it was a subtle one. My birthday came around. Gosh, I found myself dining in by myself to celebrate the day a king was born. It definitely was a very uncomfortable year for me. But I kept going because of my faith and love. That's what kept me on my feet. That's what kept me sound. No calls, no show. In that process I felt like quitting. I felt so dead inside. To be more exact, I felt so empty. But why was I focused so much on these thoughts? Was it because everyone around me had what I didn't? Did I want what they had? I had had it already. But I decided to let it go for a better future, I thought.

Sure enough I was right. Little did I know that my life was going to turn around in such an amazing way. That was when she came into the picture—the love of my life. It all happened so naturally, like it was meant to be. Sure enough it was. So my ex found out—while she still had hope. While she still believed that our love would somehow find its way back to us. I had risked it all for love. I broke her. While I felt so guilty for what I had done, my choices had hurt the girl I was with for eight years of my life. I never heard from her again.

After that, I wanted to tell her the truth. I felt she had felt that I had just replaced her or even that my love for her was not real. But it was very real. The thing here was that I had asked God for a book, and God knew she couldn't give that to me. And the one who could was standing right in front of me. But because I didn't have the knowledge I have today, I made so many mistakes and kept this all bottled inside.

And that's what leads me to this chapter. Had I told her everything when I had the chance, I would have set myself free. But because we left everything unspoken, that first love still lingered in the air between us. She was holding on to so much resentment, while I was holding on to so much guilt inside. Every chance that I would get, I would try to release it and tell the truth. But out of respect to my fiance, I always held back. Years passed, and I still had all this guilt bottled inside me—the guilt of letting her go when we had so many years invested into our relationship, the guilt of choosing Pamela over her after I had just recently met Pam, the guilt that I said bye to eight years of our relationship, and the guilt that it was just so easy for me to choose Pam over her who tolerated so much from me and loved me more than she loved herself. It was consuming me. I knew that the same was happening for her. Resentment was consuming her inside. Every chance she got to fire, she would not hesitate and fire back.

All in all this is why closure is the most important step that needs to occur between two people who have ended their relationship. You will save yourself a heartbreak. You will save yourself from hurting someone else. More importantly you will save yourself from hurting your significant other. It's almost as if you have to be transparent, even if the truth hurts. Truth doesn't always wind up to be a positive state of mind. The opposite is true as well. The truth also has negativity behind it, meaning in this situation that saying the truth, like in my story, meant she was going to resent me for it. This meant that neither I nor anyone else could take that away but time. But it was only going to be temporary. To explain more in detail, it's as if we had to end up on bad terms. So we could both have the conviction of the other person regretting their decision or just conviction to forget and move on. My story did not end up like this, and now I wish it would have. I wish she had hurt me as much as I did her so I could just have the conviction to forget and move on. But because there was no closure, the result was long term.

CHAPTER 12

Why Your Ex Keeps Coming Back

I'm pretty sure everyone can relate to finding yourself in a new relationship and your past relationship keeps on coming back. Why does this keep happening? I'm writing this for those who are having this issue right now, and it's causing friction between you and your significant other. One of the main reasons why your ex-girlfriend or boyfriend keeps walking back into your life after you called it quits is very obvious. I'm quite sure everyone has grasped this awareness. You got it: it's because they didn't do any better. They couldn't do any better, and because of that they have found themselves with regret. If only somehow they could go back to you. If only somehow they could rewind time and not have made that choice. All this leads them to have insight that they have lost someone great.

The second one is the one we fail to see, the most crucial insight we lack. We fail to see it because we believe we are perfect and never wrong. So when we see our ex knocking at our door after so many months have passed by after they have broken up with us, it is fair to say we all make this comment: "Well, if they keep coming back, that's on them. There's really nothing I can do about it."

The reality is that it's in our hands to put a stop to this. It's our duty out of respect to our current significant other and for the sake of the relationship. So what is it? It's the fact that we have sugar coated our closure or that goodbye. With this action comes the act of bravery. So the next time they reach out, you accept it, but this time you hit them where it hurts: their ego. This is when they will realize that this was it. They have lost you for good. There's no going back. There's no point in beating a dead horse. So you tell them how it really is—the truth. "Hey, you have to stop this. I no longer love you. I love Roberto. I have never loved a guy the way I love him. I thought I loved you, but I was wrong. He has taught me to love in a different way than I ever imagined. I'm growing as a person every day next to him. As for you, when I was with you, I only grew insecure about myself. With you I grew more bitter and resented my life more. I have come to realize that with you I was decaying and not respecting myself as a woman. But with him it's different. Because I know that if I want to be with him, I have to love myself and respect myself. Because how could I ever give him something I don't have? With him I find myself respecting myself beyond measure. With him I have found love, joy, and peace in my life. I'm madly in love with him. I can't tell you the time or day that he stole my heart. But I can tell you that you are my past now, and you have to stay there. So this is my goodbye to you forever. I have to go now."

CHAPTER 13

When You Prioritize Your Insecurities

You set yourself up for suffering. When you prioritize your insecurities, you leave no room for appreciating what you have in your now. But more than anything, you leave no room for love, the greatest asset there ever was in this world. Love is meant to be enjoyed. But how can you do that when you prioritize your insecurities? You can't because insecurities rob you of your confidence, and most of all they rob you of your self-love.

Acting on your insecurities will never let your love life flourish because you live a life full of doubt and feeling like you're not enough because of that person. Insecurities are what rot away love. They rob your partner of a fair chance at being in love and cherishing it. Yet by default they fall into this trap without even knowing it. So they begin to doubt the love that they are giving. They begin to question if they are enough—almost as if this is their fault and the partner with the insecurities is the victim. So now they themselves are insecure. Insecurities are contagious, like rotten fruit. You put that rotten fruit within the bunch that's not rotten, and guess what happens. Everything begins to rot.

It's important to know that if you do prioritize your insecurities in your dating world, your relationship will eventually die out. But more importantly you will emotionally affect your partner in a negative way.

And what is the secret to this world? To emotionally impact others, is to have the most expensive currency there is—positively, of course.

CHAPTER 14

Tolerance Is One Thing, but Tolerance and Self-Respect Are Another

Nowadays love gurus and love experts will inform you of the secret to making a relationship or a marriage last. It's so damn good and catchy. Here it is: the reason our grandparents and parents made it all the way with each other is because they tolerated each other's behavior and actions. That's the secret—that they would forgive and tolerate each other. It really makes a lot of sense because none of us are perfect. We have imperfections in our behavior and actions.

But now in this modern dating world, if you do one thing wrong, one minimal thing, that makes our significant other upset. Guess what. You're being replaced. Because nowadays it's so easy to be replaced. But the point here is that people won't tolerate their lovers.

So if the key to success in a marriage is tolerance, as these experts say, then I go ahead and take that advice and apply tunnel vision with it. Then my marriage has to last to the end of days, right? But what if they are misbehaving and not respecting you with their behavior, and you follow the advice of tolerating? What then? Yes, the relationship won't end, but what does? What does end is your love for the individual. It burns out. Because if there's no respect, there's no love. We know that.

So basically you're telling me that my grandparents lasted this whole time together but with a cost? That comfort is more powerful than love? So because it was all they knew and were taught, that's all they can give to each other. But they were sacrificing one powerful emotion, one emotion that defines us all. It's what we all want and need at the end of the day: love. They were sacrificing love without even knowing it. Because you can either tolerate your significant other's disrespectful behavior—how they were taught to do—or now you can tolerate and follow that advice but correlate it with self-respect. What I mean is that you can make your marriage last to eternity, but which would you rather have it with? with love in it? Or just be able to say and show the world that it's possible to marry someone and make it all the way to the end of days? Yet you leave out the part telling everyone that there's no love because you followed the advice of just tolerating them.

The moral of the story is that, yes, you can make your marriage last like our grandparents' did. But if you make it last by tolerating their disrespectful behaviors and actions, you will be left with no love for each other—just comfort and the privilege to say you and your significant other made it to the end of days. But if you choose to marry your significant other and you apply both tolerance and self-respect to the relationship, you will be able to make it to the end of days with them and with love in it. Why? Because not only did you tolerate them, but you also correlated tolerance with self-respect. And what is self-respect? It's love.

About the Author

Roberto Sanchez Jr. is a self-proclaimed early bird by morning and a gym rat by night. But through it all, he is a child at heart. Roberto has sought balance his entire life, which led him to his purpose to break the cycle of suffering in his life. Having Pamela, the love of his life, the woman that has given him a book due to her imperfections, by his side motivates him and fuels his passion for living. Despite the pain and heartbreak that he has endured from loving and losing, Roberto's mantra is that he would rather have loved than not loved at all.

www.ingramcontent.com/pod-product-compliance
Lightning Source LLC
LaVergne TN
LVHW010438070526
838199LV00066B/6069